# THE GOD WHO ANSWERS US

## TINA DOWNER

# THE GOD WHO
# ANSWERS US

Cover design by: Art Painter

Printed in the United States of America

*I would like to dedicate this book to all of
my children and grandchildren.*

# CONTENTS

# INTRODUCTION

God usually answers in four or five different ways. Yes, no, wait and I will if you will. We at times may think that He didn't answer us but it could have been an answer we didn't expect or even realize.

 Most of the stories I want to share with you are true personal life stories of amazing miracles and un-expected answers I and others received from God. Maybe one of the stories in this book will be an an-swer to one of your prayers.

# JESUS HELP!

For many years after my divorce, I was the sole provider and caretaker for my 3 young children. However, there were times when they would live with their dad. After living with my ex-husband for a few years, my oldest son David, decided he wanted to come stay with me again.

My youngest daughter Christina came along on the trip to pick him up, with the Michigan highways mostly clear but snowing when we arrived. We loaded his stuff including a dirt bike which we carefully put in the back of my pick-up truck and began our return trip home.

By the time we were on the road again dusk had fallen along with the temperature, and suddenly my truck was spinning out of control. Without seeing it I hit an area of black ice, and not being able to regain control we slid down the embankment. I did not know what to do. I cried out to the Lord at that moment, just two words, Jesus Help!

We slid down the embankment about fifteen feet and the truck stalled. I tried and failed to get back up the embankment. I know it is best to stay with your vehicle, if you get in an accident, but we left the truck in search of help. We came upon a gas station and called for a tow truck to get us back on the road.

On the way back to our truck, we noticed several other vehicles all the way down the embankment and flipped over. We did not lose anything out of it, and the dirt bike was still intact. I had absolutely no damage to my truck! I believe God was watching over us that day. From the looks of those other vehicles, it could have been a lot worse! My desperate prayer was answered!

*Discussion moments*

*Have you found yourself in a similar situation?*

*What was the first thing you did?*

# THE TORNADO

We were watching the news and saw that a tornado in Florida was headed towards our daughter, Kristin. A hurricane had come earlier that week, spawning tornadoes throughout the state. My husband and I prayed for her protection that night as we were going to bed. I usually place a hedge of protection around my children daily, and speak a scripture verse over them which says, Psalm 91:11-12 "For he will command his angels concerning you to guard you in all your ways; they will lift you up in their hands, so that you will not strike your foot against a stone." NIV

While praying, my husband Rick saw a vision of a big female angel standing by Kristin's apartment building. This angel was wearing a long white gown and had to be at least 20 feet tall! She stood with her arms outstretched, holding back the winds from reaching the apartment building. The gray storm clouds were rolling all around. The wind whipped around this angel, but she stood strong against the fierce winds! We were not worried about our daughter and slept well that night.

We received a call from Kristin the next day. A tornado had touched down near her apartment area. She told us how other apartment complexes close to her had gotten damaged by the winds, but nothing happened to her building.

God answered our prayer and kept our child safe!

*Discussion moments*

*What scripture verses do you pray over your children?*

*What protection prayers have been answered for you?*

# REVISITING THE OLD RUGGED CROSS

The last word that Jesus spoke when he was on the cross was, "It is finished." According to the Gospel of John, Jesus had completed the work He was sent to do.

What did Jesus do on the cross? I am not a pastor or preacher. I have not gone to seminary or bible college. I am just a lay person. I have heard pastors speak about the cross and the power of the cross, and there have been songs sung about the power of the cross. It did not really hit me until I received my own revelation of the power of the cross, which I would like to share with you.

I believe and now know, that the cross is an extremely powerful place, and I will never look at the cross the same way again.

Men who were to be crucified, had to carry their own heavy beam, weighing 30 to 40 pounds. According to the Gospel of Matthew 27:32, Simon of Cyrene was forced to help carry Jesus's cross. I have pictured in my mind, what the cross would look like. It would not be a smooth beam, but I think of it, as a tree limb beam with the bumpy bark. Although Jesus is no longer there on the cross, when I visit, I will pray and lay things down. Sometimes I think of touching the cross, touching the bark and pulling my hand back, looking at my hand, I see the blood on it. It is the blood that was shed for you and me. The blood that heals us and washes away our sins. The old, rugged cross. It is a messy place. A place where I know that I can go for healing, or at times forgiveness, or maybe when I am dealing with something difficult in life, that I do not know what to do about.

The Cross of Jesus Christ is where He did everything for us. He laid his life down, so that we could live. He carried and bore our diseases and sicknesses. He took all our sins. We are forgiven, we are healed, and we are free because of what He has done for us. Jesus Christ defeated the devil right there when He died for us. I know that you have heard this before.

The revelation is, that we need to visit and revisit the cross of Christ. When we do, we need to lay our sins down and leave them there at His cross. Colossians 2:13-15 "When you were dead in your sins and in the circumcision of your sinful nature, God made you alive with Christ. He forgave us all our sins, having canceled the written code, with its regulations, that was against us and that stood opposed to us; he took it away nailing it to his cross. And having disarmed the powers and authorities, he made a public spectacle of them, triumphing over them by the cross." NIV

We need to bring all our sicknesses and diseases to the cross and realize that He already dealt with diseases and sicknesses on His cross. He already carried it, why do you think that you need to carry it? Leave it all there, at the cross. He wants you to be healed, why else would it say, "He himself bore our sins in his body on the tree, so that we might die to sins and live for righteousness; by his wounds you have been healed." 1 Pet. 2:24

The old, rugged cross. It is a messy place, but it is a place where the work gets done. It is a powerful place, a place where I know that the Lord will meet with me. His presence is there, because I go there, to deal with those hard things in life. I lay all my burdens down there. Sometimes, I need to confess my mess ups, and my sins there. Other times, I picture bringing people who I am praying for, with me. I go there, to ask Jesus to help me to forgive someone.

I recently had to go there again, to ask Jesus to help me forgive. I really did not want to, but I knew that I needed to, even though I felt that they had done me wrong. I brought this person with me in my mind, and just told Jesus about it, and all the anger that I had for this person left me right away. Then I was able to forgive. I left that anger and person, there at the cross. I do not need to carry it anymore!

Jesus was such an example to us. He did everything for us on His cross. We also, need to go to His cross again, and as many times as needed, until we have laid it all down. We are forgiven, because of what He has done for us on His cross! We are healed, because of what He has done for us, on His cross!

If you want to experience for yourself, the power of the cross, you need to imagine going to the cross. You need to picture the cross in your mind, and you must think about what Jesus did there. This is where you thank Him for doing everything for you.

"Lord I thank you for going to the cross for me. I thank you for shedding your blood for me. I thank you for taking all my sins and for taking all my sicknesses and diseases upon you. I thank you for forgiving me and healing me."

Next, I lay down those people and whatever issues that have been bothering me. Then I would go into more detail about everything. Just talk to Him!

Jesus wants you to come and talk to Him. He is waiting for you to do that today. Expect a powerful experience when you lay everything down. Leave it all there at the foot of the cross. Do not take it back up again.

*Discussion moments*

*Have you had a revelation of the cross of Christ or a revelation of the power of the cross?*

*Do you think it is important to visit the cross more than once?*

# A TALE OF TWO CROSSES

The first cross is the Cross of Christ which I wrote about in the previous chapter. It is a powerful place to go when you need that extra something to help with life in general! Jesus will meet you there especially when work needs to get done.

The second cross is the cross that you carry. I really have not heard much spoken on this. So, from my own revelation, Jesus told us to take up our cross and follow Him. What I have heard some say is, that the cross we carry is a burden. I simply cannot agree with that because Jesus would not give us burdens to carry. He is the One who has already carried all our sins, sicknesses, all our burdens. Matt. 11:29,30 "Come to Me, all you who labor and are heavy laden, and I will give you rest. Take My yoke upon you and learn from Me, for I am gentle and lowly in heart, and you will find rest for your souls. For my yoke is easy and My burden is light." NKJV

The cross that I carry is light and it reflects what my Lord has done for me. The cross that I carry, is not just an empty cross, it says something. The cross of Jesus said on it, "The King of The Jews." My cross says, "Daughter of the King, forgiven, healed, and free" because that is what Jesus has done for me. He has healed me many times, physically and emotionally and He continues to heal. He has forgiven me of much and He continues to forgive. I am free because He has removed every burden and destroyed every yoke in my life! My cross reflects what He did for me, and it is not a burden to carry. It is more of an honor to carry it.

*Discussion moments*
*What do you think it means to carry your own cross?*
*What would your cross say?*

# SONS AND DAUGHTERS OF THE KING

I worked on my family genealogy a few years ago. I learned a lot of it from my cousin, Don, who spent many years working on it. When he gave me the information, I wanted to find out more. I wanted to find out where our family came from. Where did it all start? What country was the motherland? What year did they come across?

I found out that my family, on my mother's side, came across from France, into Canada in the 1600's. It was interesting that my 9x great grandfather was a farmer. He was a real pioneer. During the 1600's, France was trying to protect their colony in Canada. It was the province of Quebec. The French government sent many military men there, along with workers and farmers. It was such a harsh rugged place with Indian wars and wild animals, that most women did not want to be there. The governor of Quebec asked the King Louis of France, if he could get some women there, so that they could get their colony established better. The King agreed to send some women.

At that time, King Louis XIV decreed any young woman who was an orphan, could go to the new land and they would receive a dowry from the King. (This is a true story, really!) About 800 women signed up to go, and each was given a dowry, from the King of France. They also received a title, which was "daughters of the king." These young pioneering women would learn how to care for children and their soon to be husband's, while they were aboard their sailing ships. When they arrived, the men in the area would line the docks, to choose who they wanted to marry.

My brave 9x great grandmother, Catherine, was on one of those ships, and she married Mathuran, the farmer. They had 5 children. So, my family helped to populate the province of Quebec. The interesting part of the story is the title. Most people do not think much of a title. But to me, a title that says, "Daughters of the King" is special. It does not mean that I have royal blood. I do not, but I do have a title, that cannot be denied and that means something to me. The special thing about a title is, that it gives you some form of authority.

If you have asked Jesus into your life, and accepted him as Lord and Savior, then you also have a title. You are a part of the kingdom of God, where Jesus Christ is the King of Kings, and your title is, Son or Daughter of the King! Start calling yourself Son or Daughter of the King. It will sound foreign at first, but after saying it a few times to yourself, you will get used to it.

When you know who you are in Christ, you begin to pray differently, there seems to be more power in the prayers that are prayed, because you have the confidence in knowing who you are. Imagine when you pray, take your place as a Daughter or Son of the King, and pray with that new authority. You are so much more than a child of God! Being a child of God, is great. Being Sons and Daughters of the King, gives you authority and identity when you pray, to make decrees and declarations! Begin to declare who you are in Jesus Christ.

To declare means to officially make known. To me, it means that I believe something so deeply that I am going to speak it out loud.

God's Word, the Bible is true, and you really cannot go wrong when you are speaking His Word back to Him when you are in a prayer setting!

God spoke everything into existence. His Word is enormously powerful. It is the most powerful force in the universe! Just as God's Word is powerful, the words that we speak are powerful and important too. Proverbs 18:21 "Death and life are in the power of the tongue and they that love it shall eat the fruit thereof." KJV Matthew 12:36-37 "But I tell you that men will have to give an account on the day of judgement for every careless word they have spoken. For by your words, you will be acquitted, and by your words you will be condemned." NIV

You can bless or curse yourself and others with your words, so be careful with what comes out of your mouth! Declarations are powerful because you are agreeing with the word that you are speaking.

Here are some declarations to start with.

I am a daughter (son) of the King. I am forgiven, I am loved, I am saved, I am set free. I am healed.

I am casting all my cares on him, for He cares for me. 1 Peter 5:7

I trust in the Lord with all my heart, and I lean not on my own understanding. Prov. 3:5

I delight myself in the Lord and He gives me the desires of my heart. Ps. 37:4

In all my ways I acknowledge Him, and He directs my path. Col. 1:11

I can do all things through Christ who strengthens me. Phil 11:14

Great is the peace of my children for they are taught by the Lord. Is. 54:13

I will fear no evil, for you are with me Lord, your Word and your Spirit, they comfort me. Psalm 23:4

The Lord is my refuge! No plague will come near my home and He will keep me and my family safe! Psalm 91

The same spirit that raised Christ from the dead dwells in me and quickens my mortal body. Rom. 8:11

The Lord delivers me out of all my afflictions. Psalms 34:19

I am an overcomer by the blood of the lamb and by the word of my testimony. Rev. 12:11

There is no curse on my finances. Mal.3:7

The Lord will rebuke the devourer off everything that belongs to me because I am a tither! Mal. 3:11

Greater is He that is in me, than he that is in the world. 1 John 4:4

There is no lack for my God supplies all my needs according to his riches in glory by Christ Jesus. Phil.4:19

I will fear no evil, for you are with me Lord, your word and your Spirit, they comfort me. Psalm 23:4.

The Word of God is forever settled in heaven. Psalm 119:89

I let the peace of God rule in my heart and I refuse to worry about anything. Col. 3:15

I will not let the Word of God depart from before my eyes, for it is life to me for I have found it

and it is health and healing to all my flesh. Proverbs 4:21,22

No weapon formed against me shall prosper for my righteousness is of the Lord. Is 54:17

I take the shield of faith and I quench every fiery dart that the wicked one brings against me.

Eph. 6:10

The devil flees from me because I resist him in the name of Jesus. James 4:7

I do follow the Good Shepherd and I know His voice and the voice of a stranger I will not

follow. John 10:4

My God is able to do exceedingly abundantly above all that I ask or think. Eph. 3:20

I am thanking you Lord for providing healing for me. By faith I receive that provision now in Jesus' name. I agree with and believe your Word which says, "by His stripes I was healed" and I command my body to line up with the Word of God. I speak to the individual parts of my body (that are in need right now) my brain, heart, lungs, skin, bones, blood, muscles and joints, and all organs.

Jesus Christ bore my sickness and carried my pain on His cross. God has sent His Word to heal me, and I declare I am healed. So, body, line up right now, with the Word of God in the name of the Lord Jesus Christ.

Your Word will not return to you void, but it will go forth and accomplish what you have called it to do. Isaiah 55:11

*Discussion moments*

*Do you believe that you are a Son or a Daughter of the King?*

*What are you going to do with your title?*

*Why is it important to rise up and walk in the authority of who you really are?*

# EXPECTING

"But this man, after he had offered one sacrifice for sins forever, sat down on the right hand of God From henceforth expecting till his enemies be made his footstool." Heb.10:12,13 KJV

Expecting, really stood out to me in this verse. Way back years ago, when you aligned yourself with a family or friend, you would declare that their friends would be your friends, and their enemies would be your enemies and vice versa. On that note, God's enemies are my enemies!

Who are God's enemies? Satan and his hordes of demons are. How will His enemies be made a footstool?

I believe that when I pray and need to come against

something that is attacking me, I need to bind it up with the Word of God and send it under the feet of Jesus. As Jesus mentioned in Matthew 16:19 "What we bind on earth will be bound in heaven." Also, to ask the Lord to release what has been taken from us during the time of attack.

For many years in my prayer life, have not done that. I wonder if that is why, I have had to deal with those same things, over and over. Now, I pray differently, for myself and my family and my sphere of influence.

Jesus is expecting His enemies, my enemies, to be made His footstool. How? Through praying and using our authority as Sons and Daughters of the King. Jesus gave us His Word, to use whenever it is needed. Jesus used the Word after He had fasted for 40 days. "Now when the tempter came to Him, he said, "If you are the Son of God, command that these stones become bread." But He answered and said, "It is written, Man shall not live by bread alone, but by every word that proceeds from the mouth of God." Matthew 4:3-4 NKJV

It is so important to be sure that we are fully protected every day. The apostle Paul said to wear the full armor of God, and his words picture a soldier wearing a helmet, breastplate, belt, foot protection sword and shield. Eph. 6:13-18  It is all about wearing the Word of God and the Name of Jesus, keeping faith with you always to be prepared.

The devil is like a lawless gangster and the Bible –

the Word of God is what we need to use against him. We need to be like policemen to stand against him, with the Word as our weapon, just as Jesus used it, for our own lives, our health, or finances our families, our communities, our cities and our country.

We speak the Word over our homes when sickness or disease tries to enter. Psalm 91:10 "No evil shall befall you, nor shall any plague come near your dwelling." NKJV

Instead of saying, Yes, the family has the flu, we should be saying, "according to the Word of God, no plague shall come near my dwelling, so I command flu viruses, sickness and disease to get out of my house and I will call forth healing in its place. Sickness and disease are not allowed here, and I will send it under the feet of Jesus! Jesus already dealt with sickness and disease on His Cross."

We have the right to send whatever is attacking us, under the feet of Jesus. Such as depression, addictions, anxiety, and financial problems. Whenever you feel that you are being attacked in some way, you have that authority, as Sons and Daughters of the King, against anything the devil tries to attack you with!

Even though the devil was defeated at the cross, he still roams the earth seeking whom he may devour. Our Bible tells us that in the end the devil will be thrown into the lake of fire. Rev. 20:10. In the meantime we need to enforce the Word of God for ourselves and our families and stay within the sphere of our influence.

We all have a sphere of influence which is usually our family and friends. The promises and scriptures in the Bible tell us what to do and proclaim when we come under attack. As we stand up to the devil he will flee. Stand up now, Sons and Daughters of the King!

*Discussion moments*

*Have you ever wondered what this Hebrews 10:12 meant in the Bible?*

*Do you think that once we have battled something that has attacked us, we should send it under the feet of Jesus?*

# THE VOICE

My daughter, Christina went through a phase in high school, with a crowd that stayed out late and liked to party. One specific night, it was so strong on my heart to pray for her. I asked the Lord to protect her and keep her safe. Help her with the choices that she was makes with her friends.

On that night she was in an accident. She was in the very back of an Explorer with no seat belt when they crashed. The next thing she remembered was a woman's vice saying "Christina, you need to get up and get out of the car." Opening her eyes, she realized she was in the middle seat. Her neck hurt bad. She thought she was paralyzed. There was no one else in the vehicle. She heard screams in the distance.

Unable to move, she heard the voice again, more firmly say, "Here, take my hand." Only an arm came through the side door. Christina grabbed it, and slowly got up, to notice the vehicle nose down with the rear in the air, and half filled with water. She stepped out into the water and looked around. Her friends had left her in the field and were halfway down the dirt road. No one was physically close enough to have just helped her out of the vehicle. She only saw an arm and heard a female voice. The whole left side of her face felt on fire. She touched it and saw the blood. She ran to catch up with the others and found some of them bleeding too. Everyone was okay and made it home that night. But who helped my daughter? I believe the Lord answered my prayer by having one of His angels show up!

*"For He will give his angels charge over you to keep you in all your ways." Psalm 91:11*

*Discussion moments*

*Have you heard of an angel showing up to help someone in your family?*

*How has God answered your prayers?*

# HOW TO MOVE A MOUNTAIN IN 3 EASY STEPS

I lived in Colorado for about 12 years or so. Colorado has many mountains. In 2012 there was a forest fire that started in Waldo Canyon, near where we were living, in the mountains, and it went into the city of Colorado Springs. We had to be evacuated for 11 days, because the fire was so close to our home. Eleven days is considered a short time when looking at containment for forest fires.

During that time, we had to think fast about the important things that we needed to bring with us in case our house burned. So, we got our important papers, some photo albums, some jewelry, clothing and that was it. There is only so much room to put stuff in the vehicle, and so much time you can have, when you are on an evacuation notice. I guess we were in shock that this was happening! After the first day, I was looking at the mountain with the fire on it. I started to think about how the name of Jesus is greater than any mountain. The name of Jesus is greater than any fire. So, my husband and I drove near the mountain and prayed. I covered the mountain with the name of Jesus, and I covered the fire with the name of Jesus too! The name of Jesus is greater than any mountain that I will ever face. Peace be still to the fire and wind.

Step 1: Cover your mountain with the name of Jesus.

Philippians 2:9-11 Therefore God exalted him to the highest place and gave him the name that is above every name, that at the name of Jesus every knee should bow, in heaven and on earth and under the earth, and every tongue acknowledge that Jesus Christ is Lord, to the glory of God the Father. NIV

Step 2: Faith

Jesus said, in Matthew 21:21 "Assuredly, I say to you, if you have faith and do not doubt, you will not only do what was done to the fig tree, but also if you say to this mountain, be removed and cast into the sea, it will be done."

We start out with a measure of faith. That is why, "Faith comes by hearing and hearing by the Word of God." Rom. 10:17 The more we hear the Word of

God and learn, the more faith grows in us.

I like to go shopping. My feet were starting to hurt a lot when I would go to a few stores. I know that they say when we age our bodies age and change. I had to start using shoe inserts for arch support. At one point my feet were so sore, I got the harder plastic inserts which helped with the pain. It hurt to go shopping and I had to do something. But then I thought, I should pray about my feet. I said, "Lord, what about my feet? I believe you can heal me." And He did. I do not need to wear the hard arch supports anymore, and I can go shopping without my feet hurting. Sometimes, God will answer the simplest prayer, when all that you have to say is "Lord I believe you can, will you?" This is a simple example of faith.

When Jesus lived on the earth with us, he went about healing all measure of diseases and sicknesses. And when people would come to Him to ask for healing for themselves, or a friend or family member, Jesus would say "According to your faith let that be unto you." I have often wondered why He said it like that to the people. All the accounts in the Bible show that they were all healed, right away.

Matt. 8:5-13 A centurion came to Jesus pleading with Him for the sake of his servant, who was paralyzed. Jesus said I will come and heal him, but the centurion said he was not worthy for Jesus to come under his roof. He asked Jesus to just speak a word, and his servant would be healed. Jesus said as you have believed so let it be done for you. And his servant was healed that same hour.

In other scripture it says do you believe. Matt. 9:28-30 And when he had come into the house the blind men came to Him. And Jesus said to them, "Do you believe that I am able to do this?" They said to Him, "Yes Lord." Then he touched their eyes, saying, "According to your faith let it be to you." And their eyes were opened. NKJV

Sometimes it can be so simple. "Lord I'm having a problem with _____. I believe you can heal me. Will you?" and He did it for me, just like that!

Step 3: Speak to the mountain and command it to move.

Jesus told us to talk to our mountain in the previous step. The disciples woke Jesus when he was sleeping in a boat, because they thought they were all going to drown, because of the storm. "Lord save us, we are going to drown." He replied, "You of little faith, why are you so afraid?" Then He got up and rebuked the winds and the waves, and it was completely calm. Matt.8:25-26

As Sons and Daughters of the King we have the authority to do this. To speak to mountains to speak to our problems and command them to move. Jesus spoke to the storms, just as we can speak to the storms in our lives also. Jesus did everything as an example to us.

When I pray for someone or even for myself, I speak to whatever it is. Someone has a heart problem I will speak to that person's heart and command it to line up with the word of God and be healed in Jesus' name. If someone has a back out of alignment, I speak to the back bones and command those bones to line up right, in Jesus' name! I pray for my own body at times and command it to line up with the Word of God. Whatever it is, speak to the problem. I have prayed about the weather at times and asked the rain to stop and it did! I have done that more than once! We had planned to go camping, and who wants to camp in tents in the rain?

Cover your mountain with the name of Jesus. Have faith in God and believe that He is able. Speak to your mountain, and command it to line up with the Word of God!

*Discussion moments*

*What mountain are you facing today that you would like to move?*

# WHEN GOD SAYS NO

God says No to us, just as any good parent does for our own good. God sees the bigger picture. We sometimes do not know the details until later.

When I was dating, I would pray over the forming relationship and ask God if this was the right person for me. I had gotten a lot of No's, and then would end the relationship. There was a time when I prayed for a guy who did not know the Lord. I really liked him. As I prayed for this man, the Lord told me No, but showed me why.

I saw in a vision a body fully stretched out on a table. It did not have any features, but the shape of a man's body. It was dark and looked lumpy like coal. I remember praying for his soul to be saved. While asking if he was the right one for me, I saw two hands move on the other side of the table. It scared me. What was that? Whose hands were on him? I knew right then that he still had an attachment, and he was not being honest with me about being involved with someone else. When I asked him about it, I found that he was still involved with his ex-wife. I ended that relationship. God does not want us to get hurt. When we ask Him something, we must be willing to accept His answer, whether it is yes, no, or wait. He will not always tell us why.

We do not know what our souls look like to God, but I got a picture of what our soul looks like within that vision. Our soul encompasses the whole shape of our body. It is black and dark until we accept that Jesus died for us on the cross. When we accept Jesus as Lord and Savior, all the black coal-looking sin gets wiped away and we are made clean. God sees us as His children. He loves us and does not want that sin on us. He made a way for us to be cleansed of it.

*The prayer of salvation*

If you have not asked Jesus into your heart, but would like to today, all you must do is make a confession out loud. Say "Lord, I admit to you that I am a sinner. I have sinned and I believe that you died on the cross for me and rose again. I invite you to come into my heart, to cleanse me from these sins. Help me turn away from them. Make me into the person that you want me to be. Please fill me with your Holy Spirit so that I will have the power I need to live for you, In Jesus name, Amen."

Then take the next step, find a church in your area which teaches you out of the Bible. Get baptized.

*Discussion moments*
*What did you do when God told you No?*

# MIRACLE ON MAIN STREET

**M**y church has small group ministries. I previously led a small group for singles and really felt that I needed to have a group for praying parents. My church allowed me to start a weekly small group. In it, we used Stormy O' Martian's book, "The Power of a Praying Parent." For about 12 weeks we would get together and pray for our children and families. Many parents received answers to their prayers. I really needed the group for myself, at that time. I needed the support and fellowship of people that would agree with me in prayer.

During this time, my daughter Christina was pregnant. She still lived with us but did not let on about the pregnancy right away. While vacationing in Colorado and suffering with morning sickness, she informed me of the news.

A few months later at an ultrasound appointment, her doctor informed her that her baby had a genetic disorder and could die before being born. If the baby made it that far, it would be a hard life for both, but the baby probably would not live long and have numerous medical complications. The doctor painted a bleak picture for Christina's baby. He was also quick to convince her to have an abortion, and that it could even be done, before leaving the hospital that day! My daughter told them that she loved this baby, and she was going to have it. She believed that God would never give her something she could not handle. Christina and her boyfriend loved each other, got married and it was a tough year for everyone. We all wanted the best for them.

Our little group looked forward to getting together each week. We were really encouraged with the answers to our prayer times, in that, it is never too soon or too late to pray for our children. I needed the extra prayer coverage for my own family, especially my daughter, and the baby. I sensed it was a powerful time for all of us.

It seemed the time went by so quickly, for my first granddaughter to be born. I felt we were prepared for her arrival. She was born perfect! There were no complications, not even a birthmark! When we cried out to God for help, He answered with a miracle! I realized that praying for the needs of others also helped release the answer that I needed for my own family. We give God the glory and praise for this great miracle!

Matt.7:12 "So then, whatever you desire that others would do to and for you, even so do also to and for them, for this is (sums up) the Law and the Prophets." Amp. Bible

"Thank you, Lord for the miracles that you do for us. Thank You for the great answers to our prayers! Help us to be a people that looks to you and your Word for our needs."

◆ ◆ ◆

*Discussion moments*

*Have you received a miracle in your life?*

# ANGELS

As we traveled by car, since my husband Rick, did not like to fly, we listened to compact disks of various pastors which we accumulated. We attended a church in Colorado Springs, and we had a compact disc that was talking about angels.

A man in the congregation, told the pastor that he saw an angel, while he was praying, during the service. The man stood there a little scared. The angel just stood in front of him, with his arms folded. The man thought for a moment that he, maybe died, because why else would he see an angel right in front of him who did not say a word?

Finally, the man asked, "What are you doing?" The angel responded, "I am waiting for you to pray so that I will have something to do." The pastor went on to say that when he prays, he hopes that his angels get a great workout, huffing and puffing.

Listening to this disc, while driving, Rick heard an audible voice say to him, "Ask the Lord to send forth His angels to plant seeds in the hearts of your children." He told me and I thought "Wow, it had to be an angel that spoke to him."

I pondered it for some time. If we ask the Lord, to send forth His angels, to plant seeds in the hearts of our children it would release the angels, to help our kids in many ways. Our children are bombarded with constant evil at every turn. Evil seeds are planted every day. If we just ask the Lord every day, to send forth His angels, it should have an impact on their lives in a good way.

When we pray, we pray to God not to angels. God is the commander in chief, and he oversees all His angels. He sends them out on our behalf, as needed. He will answer in whatever way He chooses when we pray and ask. Psalms 91:11 "For He will command his angels concerning you to guard you in all our ways; they will lift you up in their hands, so that you will not strike your foot against a stone." NIV

*Discussion moments*
*Have you heard an audible voice?*

# FAITH SPEAKS

**W**hile our children were starting to really grow up and graduate high school, Rick and I were getting uncomfortable with our jobs, our home our church and everything. We were ready for a change at that time or season in our lives. I asked the Lord why we were so uncomfortable? He told me that before a child is born, that child gets uncomfortable in order to be born. I had a dream to have a bed and breakfast in Colorado. I was about to give birth to my dream and that was exciting!

When my husband Rick and I moved to Colorado, we took a huge step in faith. We bought a house in the mountains so that I could use it to do a bed and breakfast and Rick moved his flooring business to Colorado too, since he installed flooring for many years. His father began a flooring business in Michigan when Rick was a child and passed the trade down to his children.

We started our businesses in Colorado from scratch. We prayed for wisdom and creative ideas every day. God gave us those creative ideas of how to operate our businesses. During that time what really stood out to me was that the Lord had told me to speak His Word into my situation. I asked, "what word"? and He told me "God is able." I would pray "God is able" to provide jobs to come in for my husband's business, and they would come in. I would pray over my bed and breakfast and speak "God is able" to bring in the people to stay and people would come and stay there.

Speaking "God is able" builds faith in us and speaks faith out into our situation.

I still speak God is able every single day, when I am praying for my family, my friends and myself. The full scripture verse to use is "Now to him who is able to do exceedingly abundantly above all that we ask or think according to the power that works in us." Eph. 3:20 NKJV

*Discussion moments*
*Have you taken a leap of faith in something?*

# WHAT IS IN MY HEART?

**M**y ex did not pay child support. I was angry with him for many years because I felt like he manipulated the court system. He was ordered to pay a small amount, of $25 a month, for all three children.

The Lord provided me with a good job, that helped me support myself and my children. Both my ex and I had gotten re-married. When the Friend of the court finally found him, they required he pay his child support in the amount of $25,000.

By this time, the youngest was about to graduate high school and the rest of my children were living on their own. When I talked to them about it, they wondered why I would not just let it go.

It was because I felt that he owed me. He owed me a lot and needed to pay for it. I did not want to let it go. I had raised these children by myself with hardly any help from him.

Our daughter was getting married. My ex was at the reception and I could not even talk to him.

I did not want to, but my children continued to bug me about letting it go.

Finally, I prayed about it and asked the Lord what I should do. He showed me my heart. It was a forgiveness issue. I thought I forgave him, but I did not. My heart still said that he owed me more than he could ever pay back. It was not the money issue. Even if he paid the entire $25,000, it would not be enough. He owed me more, for my hurts, for my broken heart.

When I saw my evil heart, I realized I had to forgive him of everything. I had to let it all go and let him go. I wanted to completely release him from everything I was holding onto. I wrote him a letter. As I wrote, I cried a lot. (I think that tears are a form of release.) I told him that I forgave him for everything, and I was releasing him from any child support that was due. I hoped that he would forgive me too. The Friend of the Court Office received a letter from me stating that I wanted to cancel all proceedings, and no longer wanted to pursue the child support money owed.

My children informed me that when their dad got the letter, he cried too. He also forgave me. At the next wedding, we were able to talk, with no anger or hurt feelings towards each other.

We had been in that same unforgiving place for so

many years. God answered and healed our emotions and hearts so we could move forward in our lives. You really cannot move on, if you are holding on to someone or holding something against them.

Forgive and you shall be forgiven and released.

◆ ◆ ◆

*Discussion moments*

*Have you forgiven someone after many years of holding on?*

*Did you experience a release in your life, and saw that you could move forward now?*

# THE SCARY DREAM

I had a dream that I will never forget. It has changed the way. In my dream, we were driving through a bad part of town. My van was packed full of people on a mission to help someone. Suddenly, we stalled in the middle of the road. A group of people started towards us with baseball bats in hand. While these furious people were beating on the windows and sides of the van, I was in the back seat calling upon the name of the Lord, my God for help. I felt a hand come behind the vehicle and push us further down the road to safety.

This dream scared me awake. I understood it right away. Since I was not in the driver's seat, I was not the one that was in control of my life. I am usually in the driver's seat because I enjoy driving. Usually if you have a dream about a vehicle and a road, it has something to do with you or someone else's life.

When I asked Jesus into my heart and life, I wanted Him to be in control. He is in the driver's seat!

The people that came against us are the things in life that seem as though they will overtake us. The van no longer worked on its own power, but when someone prays and calls upon the Name of God, it moves the hand of God on your behalf.

God needs and wants His people to call on His Name. He wants us to ask for His help. I know that our prayers can move the hand of God.

God answered my prayer in the dream by moving His hand to push us to safety!

Jeremiah 33:3 "Call to me and I will answer you and show you great and mighty things that you do not know." NKJV

"Lord I thank you that you give us dreams and visions like in Joel 2:28-29,32" "And it shall come to pass afterward that I will pour out My Spirit upon all flesh; your sons and your daughters shall prophesy, your old men shall dream dreams, your young men shall see visions. And also, on my menservants and on my maidservants, I will pour out My Spirit in those days...And it shall come to pass that whoever calls on the name of the Lord shall be saved. For in Mount Zion and In Jerusalem there shall be deliverance." NKJV

*Discussion moments*

*Have you ever had a dream that either scared you awake, or that you remember and believe it should have a meaning?*

*Did you understand that dream's meaning right away?*

# HOSPITAL PRAYER

**M**y husband Rick was new at praying out loud for people. Well, he was a new Christian and had a servant's heart. He worked 3 jobs when I met him, one was as a volunteer fireman.

Rick's mom was sick and ended up in the hospital. She had a serious infection. We had to get suited up with the mask and paper robes and gloves just to come into her room to visit her, since she was so contagious. We wanted to let her know that we cared about her. It was around Christmas time and I gave her a small light up tree, because she really loved Christmas time. She really missed being home, because she loved to decorate the house with her angels and trees. She had been there a few weeks already, and she was not getting any better. I just thought we should go and touch her and pray for her.

Rick and I held her hand and I asked if we could pray for her, and she told us yes. I prayed a simple prayer and asked Jesus to heal her and take that sickness off her and make her well again. Rick agreed with the prayer and we all said Amen.

As we left Rick seemed unusually quiet. When we were in the elevator he said, "I don't know what to make of this, but I saw something when you were praying." I said, "What did you see, tell me." "He said, as we were praying for mom, I saw her body move up above the bed, and then some black stuff came out of her, and then her body went back into the bed." I said, "Well I think that the black stuff was the sickness leaving her body, because we just prayed and asked Jesus to heal her."

This was the first time Rick saw anything in the spiritual realm. Rick's mom was able to go home within a week! The Lord answered our prayer with a healing!

*Discussion moments*
*Have you prayed for someone in the hospital?*
*What happened?*

# A CHRISTMAS MIRACLE

O ne of our daughter's struggled hard one year. Our youngest daughter was a single parent going to school and working for an insurance company. When the commission only pay structure changed, she made a lot less than what was needed on her paycheck.

She called her dad to let him know she was about to lose everything that she put in her storage unit. It was being locked down due to non-payment for a few months. Her laptop that was necessary for school assignments was going to be repossessed. Christmas time and penniless, she was drowning in a sea of hopelessness. On the other hand, her dad really wanted to help.

During the tough economic recession, all experienced the extra money dwindle down to nothing.

All he could think to do was cry out to God for help. Together over the phone they prayed, father and daughter, asking for help. "Lord we really need some answers from you today. Please give us the wisdom that we seek you for. Help the money to come in somehow."

Within the hour she called back. She had the creative idea to call her income tax preparer. They had just started this new program where you can get your taxes done early in December and get a partial refund back right away. She would do that and have the extra money to pay off debts, and buy Christmas presents for her daughter. She found a lifeline of hope during her struggle. The God that answers, answered with a creative idea just in time!

❖ ❖ ❖

*Discussion moments*
*Have you felt so hopeless?*
*What did a timely prayer do for you?*

# I'VE FALLEN AND
# I CAN GET UP

Rick lost his footing one blustery, winter day. The top step was covered with ice, and he fell down the stairs. He cussed and then asked God to forgive him for cussing. It hurt to slip and fall. Not just your body, but your pride. Right then, he got a strong urgency to call our daughter, Jen. She was a missionary on a Youth with a Mission base in Arkansas. He told her how he had just fallen down the stairs, but what God told him while he was picking himself up off the frigid ground was, "Even when you fall or fail, do not give up. No matter how many times you may fall, no matter how hard or how much it hurts. Keep on going! Keep on picking yourself up."

Little did he know that Jen was going through some

hard things at that time. We do not know what all she was going through, but God knows, and that phone call really touched her. Sometimes, He uses us to be the answer to another person's need. It was years later when Jen mentioned that phone call she received, and we knew that it made a difference in her life at that time. It is amazing how sometimes just a phone call can make a world of difference to someone on any given day.

"Lord help us to be a blessing or an answer to someone in need."

*Discussion moments*

*Have you been an answer to someone's need during a phone call?*

*Even when you fall or fail*
*Do not give up.*
*No matter how many times you may fall.*
*No matter how hard,*
*Or how much it hurts,*
*Keep on going,*
*Keep on picking yourself up!*

# 4 THINGS TO PRAY FOR OUR CHILDREN

**M**any years ago, I learned the importance of releasing my children to the Lord. When they were young, I did not know what to do about some of the things they did, or the fights they had with each other. Why couldn't they just get along? I asked the Lord to help me and to help them get along with each other. He said to me, "They are my children too, and I love all of my children."

I had a picture in my mind, that I was holding onto them so tightly, that nothing was going to hurt or touch them. I then realized I was trying to take care of them and do everything on my own. I had not released them to the Lord until that day. I said, "Okay, these are your children too. I release them to you. I don't want to hold on so tightly that I am not allowing you to work in their lives."

My daughter Jen became a missionary after graduating high school. She traveled all over the world, including China, Turkey, India, Mexico and many other nations. She was in Turkey in a small elevator when it quit working. Thirteen other missionaries were with her when they crashed below the ground floor, from two floors up. It was dark and dusty, but they found their way out. No one was hurt!

She was on an outreach in Mexico with some high school students when she had excruciating pain in her abdomen. The hospital in Mexico told her that they needed to perform emergency surgery on her gall bladder right away. My medical insurance had only covered her until she reached 20 years of age. It just so happened that the church had insurance on everyone that traveled in case of an emergency. Jen's surgery was covered. She had not complained of any problems before, it just came on suddenly. It would have cost three times more in America and would have been an out-of-pocket expense. We did not have that kind of cash just laying around.

She had just arrived home two weeks before the devastation of 911. She could have been delayed in New York or who knows where, coming from outside of the country. I am saying this because if I did not release my children when they were young, she might not have done all the things that she has been able to do. I had the freedom to release her. It gave her the freedom to ask the Lord what He wanted her to do. I would have worried a lot had I never released her into God's hands, but I knew that He would take good care of her.

The four things that I pray for my children are:

1. "Lord, I place a hedge of protection around all of my children and grandchildren. Your Word says that You will give your angels charge over us to keep us in all of our ways." PS. 91:11

2. "Lord, I ask you to continue to send forth your angels to plant seeds within the hearts of all of my children and grandchildren. Your Word says that all your children will be taught by the Lord and great will be your children's peace." Is. 54:13 "I also ask for this great (shalom) peace to come forth for each one."

3. "Lord, I continue to release all my children and grandchildren to you, because they are your children too, and you love all of your children." 1 John 3:1

4. "Lord, I continue to speak your Word over my family that, My God is able to do ex-

ceedingly, abundantly above all that we ask or speak, according to the power that works within us." Eph. 3:20

I do not always know what my children are going through. I know that prayer changes things for our good. I know that God answers our prayers. I pray these 4 prayers daily. When someone is traveling, I ask God for some extra angels to protect them, so that they can get to their destination safely.

*Discussion moments*
*Do you have certain scripture verses that you pray for your children and family daily?*

# THREE IN
# ONE DAY

Rick was self- employed in the flooring business. His dad taught him everything he knew. When he began his own business, he had a recurring dream about a lion chasing him and eating him. He would wake me up and I would pray for him and would command the enemy to stop attacking him in his dreams. He was then able to sleep. The Lord blessed him in his business in Michigan. When we moved to Colorado, we moved his business there too.

We started with nothing but a prayer. I would pray these prayers every day. "God is able to bring people that need my husband's business services. God can give us creative ideas on how to do business here. God is able to give us divine appointments with people that can help us with our business. God can put us in the right place at the right time. God is able to bless the work of my husband's hands and cause us to prosper." Praying "God is able," really causes faith to rise. It will also bring God's Word into our lives and situations.

At this time, I went through the phone book and gave my husband a list of flooring stores he could visit, and he received many jobs from these creative ideas.

About a year later one of his business acquaintances had parted ways with him and it ended on bad terms. Then others followed. One day, while Rick prayed for his business, it was strong on his heart to ask for forgiveness of his acquaintances, even though he did not think that he did anything wrong. He went in person to one and asked the man to forgive him. This man asked Rick to forgive him as well. About an hour after leaving, he received a phone call from another person asking for forgiveness for everything that happened in their business relationship. A few minutes after that call ended, there was another asking to forgive. All of this happened within an hour on the same day because Rick decided to ask someone to forgive him.

When we pray and ask God and others to forgive us, and to help us to forgive others, we might receive what we ask for. Sometimes forgiving someone might open another door in life. Rick was doing okay in his business. After forgiving and being forgiven, it did open other doors for other business opportunities. Rick was given a rhema word that day during his prayer time. He knew that word Forgiveness was important, so he used it.

"Our Father forgive our trespasses as we forgive those who have trespassed against us. Father, please help us to forgive anyone that has done something to hurt us in any way. Also, help anyone to forgive us that we have wronged or hurt in any way. Please forgive us Lord so that we can be forgiven. Thank You."

*Discussion moments*

*Have you ever felt that urge to ask someone to forgive you when you did not feel you were wrong?*

*Have you had anyone ask you to forgive them?*

*Have you ever acted on a rhema word that you received?*

# YOUR CHOICE

Has God ever told you, it is up to you? I would ask countless times when I dated, "God is he the right one for me." I was impressed with no, many times. I have made many wrong choices in the past without asking Him first. God is our loving Father. When we ask, He tells us because, He cares. Any loving mother and father will say, "No! Don't touch that it's hot!" "No, that fell on the ground, don't eat it." Not accepting the "No" can lead to disaster and heartache.

Rick was pursuing me, and finally asked for my hand in marriage. He asked me more than one time. I wanted to bring that decision to the Lord. So, I asked, "Is he the right one for me?" I expected another "No", but I was impressed with, "It's up to you. Your choice." What? I thought I would get another no, or maybe even a yes. It is my choice? That made it harder for me. I had to decide on my own. Someone once told me that, when your relationship grows with the Lord, He will trust you to make your own choice. Marriage is a big decision. We need to continue to work at it to keep it good. I wanted some more time to get to know what he was like. Rick and I courted for a year and were married. Our life together had been one great adventure!

*Discussion moments*
*Has God told you yes, no, wait, or it is up to you when you asked Him?*

# MY MIRACLE

I worked a third shift job in a factory but was looking for something else. I was really excited about finding a part time position, as a rural route carrier with the post office. Training lasted two weeks, where I learned how to stage the mail in the boxes and get it ready for delivery.

The day came for me to learn the route I would be doing daily. I was taking the position of a lady who was going on a vacation for two weeks. Her station wagon had the steering wheel on the opposite side, which was perfect for a mail carrier. I had to practice driving my Ford Explorer from the middle seating area, while straddling the console. It was not easy delivering mail that way. At one stop, the drive was long and bumpy. I hit a big pothole and my foot slipped on to the gas pedal. A small fir tree stopped me from hitting the garage and house. The passenger side A-arm near the ty-rod, broke and my

Explorer was no longer drivable. Unable to finish my route, I had to call the postmaster and inform him of what happened. He had to finish my route that day. I was a little shaken up.

I decided the post office job would not work out for me, so they had to find someone else to fill in. I still had my factory job, which provided for my family, but had to find a ride until my Explorer was fixed.

About a month later, I was on my lunch break when I felt a pain in my rib area. The headline on top of a stack of magazines, read of a woman who overcame lung cancer, because they detected it early. She had pain in her abdomen and had her lungs ex rayed. That is when they found the cancer. It grabbed my attention, so I decided to get it checked out. I went to my doctor, told them of my pain that was not going away. My doctor was not satisfied with the x-ray results and ordered more.

I was sent for a cat scan, then an MRI. The surgeon decided surgery was necessary to remove my spleen. He thought it might be cancer. They asked me if I had fallen and remember being hurt or had any type of accident. I said no. I did not even think that when I hit that little pine tree that I might have done something to myself.

At the same time, I had people praying for me. A friend thought I had been looking tired lately. She never said anything to me, she just prayed. There are times that other people's prayers are why God carries us through.

I prayed for myself too. I could smell death near me. I would pray, "Lord, I am yours. My life is yours, whether you want me to live or die. I give my life to you. I know that life and death are in your hands, but if it is up to me, I choose life." Then the smell of death would leave. I realized that life and death are in God's hands alone.

As we give our lives to Him, it is up to Him, when it is our time to go. We can ask to live a little while longer. God answered my prayer when I said, "I choose life." He spared my life!

The mass on my spleen was not cancer, but a large blood clot. My red blood cells had formed together to stop my spleen from bleeding. It was an answered prayer, a miracle I think, because I could have bled to death at any time, before I even knew something was wrong. It was five months after the accident when I had surgery. I had been doing strenuous lifting at work. The slightest bump and I could have bled to death.

"Lord I thank you for the many answered prayers from people, who take the time to pray for us, without knowing the huge difference it makes in our lives. Thank you for the doctor's that have wisdom and knowledge of how to take care of our bodies.

Thank you, Lord, for carrying us through the hard times when we cannot pray for ourselves. We recognize that our lives are in your hands, as we give our lives to you."

◆ ◆ ◆

*Discussion moments*

*Have you had a miracle of God sparing your life?*

*Do you know someone who has had a miracle in their life?*

# THE WOMAN IN A BLUE FLOWERED DRESS

Rick felt his heart was lonely and empty. He was working three jobs, as a factory worker, part-time volunteer fireman and bartender. A single parent raising two children, and something was missing. He wanted a woman that he could spend some time with. He cried out to God.

God spoke to him and said, "Go to church and I will give you a wife." It sounded easy, but he had to juggle those three jobs and his kids. His neighbor's, Joe and Deb, invited him to their church. He was obedient and went to church that next Sunday. While he was standing in the lobby, a beautiful brunette walked by in a long, blue flowered dress. He heard God's voice again, "That is the woman you will marry." He thought to himself, "Am I hearing things?" Deep down he knew it was God.

Several weeks later he joined a small group for singles which was led by the woman in the blue flowered dress. Rick finally got the nerve to ask her out. That was the beginning of their relationship. They were married a year later. Rick had a heart to serve. He loved serving as a fireman, and he loved getting involved at the church, being a part of the usher ministry. Rick thanked God every day for his answered prayer.

◆ ◆ ◆

*Discussion moments*
*Has God spoken to you like Rick, in this story?*
*What happened when you asked for a spouse?*

# TRUST MEANS
# DO NOT WORRY

When I was about to marry, my soon to be husband Rick was concerned about having enough money for our honeymoon. About a week before that joyful day, while getting ready for work, he turned on the television and listened to Joyce Meyer talking about trusting God. Rick worked at a rubber factory at that time. Then, while driving home for lunch, a radio program featuring Dr. James Dobson, spoke of trusting God.

Back at work again, later that day, Rick needed a rag for his job. The rag box contained old t-shirts. Some had funny sayings on them, good for a laugh. While returning to his machine, he opened the t-shirt. It was white with pink and blue letters. It said, "Trust in the Lord with all your heart." Rick said out loud, in front of everyone, "All right Lord, I get it!"

It took him three times, but he finally got it. Rick received a rhema word from God which was Trust. We framed that t-shirt and hung it on our wall, I still have it!

God, at times talks to us, before we even say a word or ask a question, He already has the answer.

God answers, but are we listening? Rick was worrying and did not realize it. There was more than enough money that came in from people who attended our reception, and we enjoyed our honeymoon!

*Discussion moments*

*Have you received an answer from God before you asked the question?*

*Have you had something like this happen to you, three times in a day, so that you would notice?*

# PREGNANT WITH A DREAM

When I married my husband Rick, we went to Colorado on our honeymoon. I heard it was beautiful and I really wanted to visit. We stayed in a vacation rental mountain home by Pike's Peak, Colorado Springs. The mountains were beautiful, so full of pine trees. The smell is wonderful. I love the outdoors of Colorado. We fell in love with the area and decided we wanted to move there after our children were out of school. We set a goal of 5 years and gave it to God. His Word says. "Commit all that you do to the Lord and your plans will succeed." Proverbs 16.3 We took a vacation to Colorado every year to look at homes and land. As we looked, we would pray over them to see which one would be right for us.

I asked the Lord what type of work I would be doing in Colorado. He told me He would take care of it, so do not worry about it. One day, as I drove home from work, an idea popped into my head. Why not open a bed and breakfast? Right away I started getting information on bed and breakfasts. I love the idea of entertaining people in my home and get paid for them staying. It helps with the house payment. It takes a certain type of person to own and run a bed and breakfast. You need to be a people person, friendly, considerate, not easily offended and never grouchy or grumpy. Your attitude can be the deciding factor to get a return visit. You need to cater to your guests, but also have rules and regulations. There is always someone that will stretch you to your limit. You will not get rich from running a bed and breakfast.

During the five - year goal we did a lot of homework. We saw a lot of homes for sale, and even considered buying land to build on. It turned to be more expensive to build. I had this recurring night dream about a home in the mountains. It was a log cabin we had looked at that had five bedrooms and three baths. Our first reaction was that it was too big and too expensive. Why did I still dream of it? The time was getting closer to our goal, and I was feeling extremely uncomfortable with my factory job and finding it harder to go to work. I was uncomfortable with my home church and my family. I did not know why I felt this way. I asked the Lord what was going on. He told me that before a child is born, that child gets uncomfortable, before he is birthed, otherwise he would want to stay in the womb forever. So, not only is the mother uncomfortable, so is the child. Sometimes we get uncomfortable when God wants to move us forward into something.

I then realized I was pregnant with a dream to move to Colorado and do a bed and breakfast. Both men and women can become pregnant with a dream. I was so uncomfortable because I was about to give birth to it. We were about to take a giant leap of faith and step into the unknown. We were not afraid because where God guides you, He will provide. We had our plan and committed it to the Lord by simply praying, "Lord, we submit this plan of moving to Colorado and going into business there. We ask for success over these plans according to your will for our lives. As your Word says to "Commit to the Lord, whatever you do, and your plans will succeed." Proverbs 16:3 NIV

We inquired about the home I was dreaming about. It had gone down in price. We made an offer, and it was accepted. Before we even made the decision to move out of the State of Michigan, Rick and I discussed the importance of being on the same page with each other. We had the same dreams and goals for our lives, but if we were not in agreement with this decision, God would not answer our prayers.

Sometimes, we look back on the events of the day we get married, get all dressed up and emotional, but we forget about the bonds and the commitments that were made that day. Our prayers will not get answered until we agree again with each other. Just as you light that unity candle on your wedding day, keep that unity candle burning in your hearts every day!

"Lord, I thank you for the dreams that you give us. I thank you for birthing those dreams. I thank you for also showing us the importance of agreement and unity with our spouses. Help us have more love and unity in our marriages."

*Discussion moments*

*Have you ever been uncomfortable and or pregnant with a dream?*

*Do you pray for agreement and unity in marriage?*

# RELEASING AND THANKSGIVING

We purchased a home in Colorado, but still had one in Michigan for sale. We had renters living in it, and they were destroying it. It is hard to make 2 house payments, let alone taking care of one out of state.

I prayed and prayed for it to sell. Finally, I asked God what he wanted us to do. I felt impressed to walk around the house 7 times and pray. I called my daughter to do that for me, since she lived nearby, but she did not. When we drove back to Michigan to do repairs on the home, I walked around the house 6 times, thanking Him for allowing us to live there, and raise our children there, and for allowing us to enjoy our lives in that house, while entertaining friends and family, having graduation parties, holiday events, and special times.

On the 7<sup>th</sup> time around, my daughter drove up and asked what I was doing. I told her that I was praying for our house to be sold. She agreed with me in prayer and walked around the house with me for the 7<sup>th</sup> time. We thanked God for releasing us from it and thanked Him for the sale of it.

While driving back to our Colorado home, a friend called to let me know that she worked with a lady who was interested in our home. Within two days of getting in touch with our realtor to look at it, she decided to purchase it. Our home was sold!

I believe that sometimes God will answer us with a strong urge to pray for something. When we follow through with doing it His way, it works out. If it worked before, it does not mean it will work again in the same way. It must be what is put on our heart to do at that time, and our obedience to do it. We need to ask Him what He wants us to do, and then go and do it when we sense that urging.

*Discussion moments*

*Have you ever had a strong urge to do something that might have been inconvenient?*

*Have you had a strong urge to do something, did it, and had a great answer in return?*

# A SELFISH HEART

My sister asked me to stay an extra day to go with her to Detroit, but I did not want to. I had become so selfish, and I did not realize it until my sister needed something. It is amazing how we can get all wrapped up in ourselves until God shows up and shows us our heart. Does God talk to you like, "You want to be a blessing to me, but you can't take some time to be a blessing to someone else? You ask for it, here is your chance."

Driving to Detroit would take eight hours to drive there and back. Going through downtown and side streets we saw many abandoned schools and houses, and even whole neighborhoods. I took the opportunity to pray for the city's restoration, and for new businesses. I am glad I was able to do that. I believe God will sends us to places to have us pray for that area and use those prayers to create change. I love to do drive by prying! I expect great change for Detroit. I have heard recently of new employment opportunities coming to the area. Prayer is already being answered!

"Lord, please forgive us for being selfish with our own desires. Help us to really ask you for your dreams and your desires."

◆ ◆ ◆

*Discussion moments*
*Do you find yourself being selfish sometimes?*
*How do you respond?*

# THE BROWNIE EPISODE

My husband loved to cook and clean. I am not complaining in any way. His nickname was Chef Rick. As with any good cook, he is very particular in the kitchen. I have learned to let him do his thing and not touch anything.

When we first married, we had our own sets of cooking utensils, as with everything else when you combine two families together. I was preparing a dessert with my measuring cup set. Rick came to see how things were going, and reached for his measuring cup, and said, "Here, use this one." "What is wrong with mine? I have used it for years. It works fine." I said. I guess I had to show him it was okay to use my things too. It was the beginning of a learning experience for the both of us. Just like I learned to stay out of the kitchen. Two cooks together in the kitchen do not mesh well. I have never met a person with so much passion for cooking as him. He would get angry when his bread would not rise right, or one of the egg yolks broke when he flipped them. My cooking philosophy is, "you get what I make for you and it usually isn't perfect, just eat it anyway!"

One night, Chef Rick made a delicious roast beef dinner. The vegetables were exactly right. The meat was done to tasty perfection. We ate to our fill. The chef thought brownies sounded perfect for dessert. We watched "Dancing with the Stars" while it baked and started some coffee. They were done about half through the show. Chef got them out of the oven to cool down. At least ten to fifteen minutes passed, and I went to pour coffee. That is when I noticed a big indent in the middle of the brownies. I began slicing. It broke into small pieces but smelled delicious. The first one is always hardest to get out of the pan. It was a little gooey.

Chef Rick came in to check on them. "What happened here? You ruined them by cutting them too soon," he said. His reaction made me terribly angry. I guess I did not let them cool long enough. I thought by making his coffee and cutting the brownies, to serve him, so he could enjoy the rest of the program, without missing any of it. I decided to walk the dog. When I returned, he apologized, but I was still too angry to talk to him. He went to bed and I stayed up thinking about our marriage. I thought of all the things I disliked about him. I was too angry to sleep. That is when I cried out, "Lord, I am terribly angry with my husband right now. I need you to help me to forgive him and wipe the anger away. Stop the devil from attacking us and trying to destroy our marriage." I went to bed and the anger was totally gone! God answered! I was able to sleep and forgive my husband. The enemy will take advantage of situations and attack our marriages, especially when we concentrate on the negative things. And it usually starts with just one thought.

"Lord help us to forgive each other before the day is over. Do not allow the enemy to destroy our marriages. Wipe the anger off us."

Ephesians 4:26 "Do not let the sun go down while you are still angry and do not give the devil a foothold."

*Discussion moments*

*Have you ever thought that the devil is trying to destroy your marriage?*

*What would you do?*

# TWO MORE CHILDREN

I was spending some time with the Lord, talking to Him, He told me that he was going to give me two more children. A boy and a girl. I believed Him and I thought maybe they would be twins? Because when He told me that, I was impressed that I would have them at the same time. Sometimes the Lord will speak to you before you even say a word to Him! It was quite a few years before I met Rick.

He had two children from a previous marriage, and we became a blended family when we got married. God loves all His children and He told me about two children before I even met their dad! But it was so important that He told me that day. I sensed the importance of it. Just as the importance of Psalm 139:13-18 "For you created my inmost being you knit me together in my mother's womb. I praise you because I am fearfully and wonderfully made; your works are wonderful I know that full well. My frame was not hidden from you when I was made in the secret place. When I was woven together in the depths of the earth, your eyes saw my unformed body. All the days ordained for me were written in your book before one of them came to be. How precious to me are your thoughts, O God! How vast is the sum of them, were I to count them, they would outnumber the grains of sand. When I awake, I am still with you." NIV

For our blended family, Rick and I decided that we were not going to do his kids, her kids. We decided that we would treat all our children as one family. Rick would call and treat my son and daughters, as his own son's and daughter's. I also, would call and treat his son and daughter as my own son and daughter. That was how we felt about our family, and still do. One family!

*Discussion moments*
*Has God spoken to you about something before you even said a word to Him?*

# THE WORD

How important is the Word to you? Rom. 10:17 "So then faith comes by hearing and hearing the Word of God." Your faith gets built up by hearing the Word of God. The Word is so important to me that I put it on me daily. I wear it daily. You see, The Lord told me to take His Word with me wherever I go. So, the only way I know how to take it with me everywhere, is to wear it! There are many different things that I have learned about the Word, over time. I have gone to some different churches over the years and listened to some great pastors. Pastor Paul at Riverside church, Dutch Sheets in Colorado, Robert Henderson in Colorado, Joyce Meyer and Kenneth and Gloria Copeland, to name a few. I learned from what they taught me, over time.   These pastors' and apostles have given their lives to teach and preach God's Word to the people.

I am writing this book, because of the Word that was brought forth through these pastors, who took the time to study, and be the messenger. I have used the Word that was taught and preached, and I tell you, it works. I have seen miracles and received miracles and many answered prayers!

We all want something that will work for us, but if you do not use something that has been given to you, it will not work for you. Man shall not live by bread alone but by every Word that comes out of the mouth of God. Is. 55:8-11 "For my thoughts are not your thoughts, nor are your ways My ways, says the Lord." "For as the heavens are higher than the earth, so are My ways higher than your ways, And My thoughts than your thoughts." "For as the rain comes down and snow from heaven, and do not return there, but water the earth, and make it bring forth and bud, that it may give seed to the sower and bread to the eater, so shall my word be that goes forth from my mouth; it shall not return to me void, but it shall accomplish what I please, And it shall prosper in the thing for which I have sent it." NKJV

One day, when you realize that the Word is the most powerful force in the universe it makes sense to you. This world that we live in was created by the Word. John 1:1 "In the beginning was the word and the word was with God and the word was God." The Word is not wishy washy, but true and unchangeable. Psalm 119:89 "Forever, O Lord, Your

Word is settled in heaven." NKJV Since it is settled in heaven, it cannot be changed. The Word is true, all of it. I can rely on the Word. I believe it is true. He is faithful to keep His Word to his people. Deut. 7:9 "Therefore know that the Lord your God, He is God, the faithful God who keeps covenant and mercy for a thousand generations with those who love Him and keep His commandments." NKJV

I wear the Word on me, like it says wear the full armor of God. I wear the Name of Jesus on me. He gave me His name, as a part of the bride of Christ. I have authority to use the Word of God and the Name of Jesus. I am a Daughter of the King. We need to realize where our authority is. Our authority is in knowing Jesus Christ as our Lord and Savior. Jesus used the Word, to come against the devil and we need to do that too. He will flee from us when we stand up to him, with the Word. Those are our weapons. The Word is powerful and sharper than any two- edged sword. Some may say or even pray, "I just want something to work." The Word works. You should use it daily, by speaking it. "They over-came him by the blood of the lamb and the word of their testimony." Rev. 12:11 NIV

The Word is so powerful, that when you need direction at a time in your life for your health or for a specific situation you can ask the Lord for a Rhema Word and He will give it to you.

When we pray in agreement, the Word is so powerful that many prayers are answered. According to

Matthew 18:18 "Again I tell you that if two of you on earth agree about anything you ask for; it shall be done for you by My Father in heaven." NIV

We have grown to be a people who want instant results. We own microwaves, to have instant meals. We have computers and the internet so that we can receive answers right away. When what we need does not happen instantly, we tend to question it. Some prayers do not get answered right away. Use the Word daily, speak it out loud, take it with you everywhere you go.

◆ ◆ ◆

*Discussion moments*

*Have you said or prayed "I just want something that works!"*

*How powerful do you think the Word is?*

# ECONOMIC CRASH

W hen we brought my husband's business to Colorado, we did not have a plan b. We had so much faith that it would work. Once we were all moved in, I prayed every day about Rick's business. I spoke out loud, God, you are able to bring forth work, you are able to help us to get established here, you are able to help us in our situation." I was praying that way, because that was how the Lord told me to pray, at that time. Before we moved to Colorado, He said to me, "whatever situation you find yourself in, speak God is able, into that situation."

I found a job for myself working in a furniture store, within two weeks of moving to Colorado. We committed our work, we committed our plans, we committed all that we did to the Lord as His Word says to. Proverbs 16:3 "Commit to the Lord whatever you do, and your plans will succeed." NIV

Rick's business started to take off, and everything was going well for us. We needed furniture, so it really helped that I was working at a furniture store...I got a small discount. In the meantime, I was preparing my home to run as a bed and breakfast. When everything was in place, it took about six months, before I was able to get it up and running.

I remember when we first got our home in the mountains, my log cabin dream home, I would pray, "Lord, thank you for allowing us to live in this beautiful home, whether I am here for one day, one week, one month or one year, I will thank you, and praise you for allowing me to do this." Then I was wondering why I would pray that way, especially when I was hoping to live there for a long time. I quit praying that way but kept that thought in the back of my mind. (Uh, oh, I may not be in this house forever.) I loved it there!

Everything was going good for us the first few years. Then in the beginning of 2008, I was praying hard about everything. I did not have a new goal yet since all my previous goals were met. My husband was complaining about working hard without seeing any results. I just thought we were working hard for our future. I released my home and businesses to God, and I felt that He wanted me to sell our home now. I thought well, maybe I am wrong, but this is a strong urge to sell it this year. I told my husband about the strong urge and he agreed with me. Although, I really did not want to because I loved it so much! I told my friends and family, but I think they thought I was nuts to sell my home! It was just so strong on me to do that. I had a realtor come and drew some things up for us. Then I put it up for sale for a few days, changed my mind. I thought that I would wait until the fall or winter and then put it up, but my window of opportunity to sell closed. No one came to look at, no offers.

The economy tanked in September 2008, and we were feeling it. My husband's work stalled, and so did the bed and breakfast. There was not enough money coming in to pay all our debts. We needed a miracle! We finally decided to file bankruptcy. We did not want to, but we had no choice. We moved back to Michigan. I know that I should have followed through and tried to sell the house earlier in the year, but I did not. Sometimes, we just do not do the right thing at the right time and then suffer the consequences.

*Discussion moments*
*Have you had a strong urge to do something and did not?*

# HE CARRIES ME

Through the process of time, while I was writing this book, and putting it all together, my husband Rick had a heart attack. We did not know that he even had a heart problem. He had some blockages which required surgery. He went through that okay, but was still having trouble breathing, so we moved back to Michigan to get to a lower altitude and be around family. He passed away suddenly one evening. A sudden cardiac arrest they said. I was praying for healing all along. The church that we belong to, was praying along with us. I know that God heals. I have had many healing's and seen many healed. Some of us will receive our healing here while others will receive their healing once they get to heaven.

I knew that this was about God's timing. I did not ask God why. We were back in Michigan for only six months. I knew that it must have been his time to go, because we all have a certain time to be here, and our days are numbered. According to Job 14:5 "Man's days are determined; you have decreed the number of his months and have set limits he cannot exceed." NIV I knew that God could heal him, but he chose to take him home instead. Those of us who have lost someone, the Lord is near. Psalm 34: 18 "The Lord is near to the brokenhearted and saves the crushed in spirit."

I found for myself that, He carries us through those difficult times as we ask him to. I felt as though I was in a bubble, just going through the motions of day-to-day life. But I was being carried. Isaiah 46:4 "Even to your old age and gray hairs I am he, I am he who will sustain you. I have made you and I will carry you; I will sustain you and I will rescue you." NKJV

The great news is that we will see our loved ones again on the other side of this life if we are saved. For not everyone will go to heaven, only the ones who accept Jesus Christ as Lord and Savior. Jesus said that He was preparing a place for us and where He is, we will be also. When someone passes away, heaven prepares for their arrival. Our loved ones are in a better place and the rest of us will not know until we get there, in God's time. He is the one who holds life and death in His hands.

*Discussion moments*
*Have you experienced God carry you through a hard time?*

# THE BANQUET TABLE

Some years ago, I was praying for a missionary who was involved with Youth with A Mission. I do not recall what exactly I was praying for, other than safety and protection, but while praying, I saw a vision of the banquet room in heaven. The tables were set with white tablecloths and elegant dishes. The tables were big and wide and long. The Lord was showing me where this missionary was going to be seated. I asked the Lord where my place was going to be, and He said, "over there where the holy people are."

I wondered about that, for many years. I do not think of myself as a holy person at all! I did not know who the holy people were, that I was going to be sitting with, until this last year. Sometimes, the

Lord will tell you something, and you do not get it for years. I found out that the intercessors, are the holy people He was telling me about, since I am an intercessor.

I shared a story about the place of prayer with my fellow intercessors, and while I was sharing the importance of our place in the prayer room, that vision of the banquet room came back to me.

We all have a place and a calling on our lives. I have always gravitated towards prayer. I would ask the Lord, "Where do you really want me and what do you want me to do? Where is my place Lord?" I did not realize that I was already doing what He wanted me to do, by praying and by being an intercessor. My fellow intercessors are the holy ones that Jesus was telling me about, when I had that banquet room vision, years ago. My place is the place of an intercessor, so at the banquet room, I believe that I will be seated with my fellow intercessors. Pastor's will be seated with fellow pastors, missionaries with fellow missionaries and so on.

If you belong to Christ, are ready and waiting for the bridegroom to return for His bride, the Bride of Christ, then you have a place setting already prepared and assigned to you, at the banquet table for the wedding feast.

*Discussion moments*
*What do you think the banquet table will look like?*
*Who would you like to be sitting around you?*

# SOMETHING NEW

I feel that God is answering my prayers differently than before. Last year, in January, I was concerned with a bump on my chest, which was not going away. So, I prayed a little differently. I said, "Lord, I am concerned with this bump here. I know that you can heal me, will you?" Then, when I was done talking to the Lord, and done with my prayer time, I left the room and went into the living room and sat down. While watching TV, I felt a warmth in my upper torso going across horizontally. It continued for five or six minutes. It was so warm, and at some point, so hot, that it almost burned on the inside. I feel that something got burned off me, possibly my lungs or breast or heart area. I do not really know, but I do know that it was the Lord healing me! I had just left the room after asking Him to heal me.

I physically felt awful for about three weeks. I

think that our bodies take time to heal after having some type of procedure done, and that felt like a procedure. The bump I was concerned about ended up being a pimple that went inside. I had it removed. I could not understand why it was still there, and after experiencing a healing like I did. God did not answer my prayer the way I expected Him to, even when I was experiencing a healing that was probably greater than the tiny bump I was concerned with.

Months later, I had some pain on the inside of my leg and I automatically put some pain cream on it, and while I was doing that, I thought, why don't I pray about my leg pain? Normally if we get a headache, we take an aspirin, so any pain we experience, we use what we have available. I said, "Lord, I don't know what is wrong with my leg, it might be a pinched nerve or something because it has been hurting me for a few days now. I know that you can heal me, will you?" I felt the pain going away right away and have not had any more pain in that leg.

I feel as though God is doing something new, in how He is answering prayer, but sometimes He shows us to pray differently too. He answers when we pray in faith, believing He can help us. Not so much when we pray from a place of pain.

*Discussion moments*

*Do you think that God is answering your prayers differently?*

*What is the difference of praying with faith compared to praying from a place of pain?*

# IN PURSUIT
# OF PEACE

I asked the Lord for a better understanding of peace. Peace is something that we can feel. The first time I felt peace, I was at work and just felt an overwhelming sense that everything was going to be okay. Everything I was concerned about, or worrying over did not matter, because it was going to be alright somehow. It is like when someone says to you, "Don't worry, I got this." (And you just know that they do.)

I have been praying and declaring this verse daily, for many years, "All your children will be taught by the Lord and great will be your children's peace." Is. 54:13 NIV. The significance has been on the Lord teaching my children, but I was somehow bypassing the second part about their peace. I would pray for their peace but did not emphasize it as much as the first part of that verse. Yay, the Lord is going to teach my children and they will have peace. I pray for people to have peace a lot. So, I use Peace during prayer times, but I needed a deeper understanding of it.

"Lord what is this peace?" Over the years I have heard messages on the peace of God, but sometimes, either during a church service, or at home the Holy Spirit helps to define it better. It seems to be a lot more than what I ever thought it was. Our English language does not define the word peace well. We have to look it up in the Hebrew language to get a better understanding of it.

The Hebrew word for peace is Shalom. Shalom can be a greeting or a farewell. Jesus said, "Peace be unto you," in the gospels. "Peace I leave with you; my peace I give to you; not as the world gives do I give to you. Let not your heart be troubled neither let it be afraid." John 14:27 NKJV

Peace is what everyone wants and seeks for in their lives. Shalom peace is wholeness, prosperity and harmony, safety, happiness, and success. This shalom peace is a powerful blessing to pray over people. It is wanting you to be completely whole, happy, secure and prosperous. It is the absolute best blessing that you can give to someone. Nothing left out. I am still learning of this powerful force called peace. It is so much more than I thought, and even more powerful.

Philippians 4:6-7 "Be anxious for nothing, but in everything by prayer and supplication, with thanksgiving, let your requests be made known to God; and the peace of God, which surpasses all understanding, will guard your hearts and minds through Christ Jesus." NKJV This is usually the verse, that pops into my mind first, when I think about peace. I think that I got stuck on the part that says, "His peace surpasses my understanding," and I did not try to learn more about it.

When the disciples were in chaos and thought they were going to drown in Mark 4:39 How powerful was it, when Jesus rebuked the wind and spoke to the sea, "Peace be still!" and the winds ceased and there was great calm. NKJV Jesus spoke to the winds and the waves and they had to calm down. Sometimes He calms the storm and sometimes He calms us down.

Jehovah Shalom is one of the names of God from the Old Testament. It means "The Lord is Peace." When we can grab ahold of the thought that one of the names of our God is Peace, we can try to understand that His desire is for us to have His Peace, and His Peace is immensely powerful, because everything about our God is powerful. The more that we seek Him, the more we find out about Him.

He wants us to have His great Peace. Just as we are told to pray for the Peace of Jerusalem and to pray for the Peace of Israel, that same peace will be on us too. If you understand how the Word of God works, His promise to Abraham was that He would bless those who blessed him (Abraham and his family), and He would curse those who cursed him. God's Word is true today as well. So those of us who would bless Israel, will be blessed and those of us who curse Israel will be cursed. Be careful with your words, and pray for the peace of Israel, and pray for the peace of your nation and yourself also, because we all really want this Shalom kind of Peace, which brings prosperity, healing, restoration, happiness, provision, security, mentally, physically, emotionally with nothing left out. Honestly, when I used to pray for the peace of Israel, I thought that I was just praying for their borders to be safe and secure. Shalom peace is so much more than security. It concerns the wellbeing of the people and of their culture.

God, from the beginning of time wanted this peace for His people, and still does today. This completeness, wholeness, restoration, happy and prosperous, shalom. He wants the absolute best for you!

The Jewish culture has learned of Shalom at an

THE GOD WHO ANSWERS US

early age. They practice it every day greeting you with Shalom, and weekly during Sabbath. I have not learned about it because we do not greet people with Shalom here in the U.S.

Jesus Christ was born Prince of Peace. Isaiah 9:6 "For unto us a Child is born, unto us a Son is given; And the government will be upon His shoulder. And His name will be called Wonderful, Counselor, Mighty God, Everlasting Father, Prince of Peace." NKJV Luke 2: 13,14 "And suddenly there was with the angel a multitude of the heavenly host praising God and saying: "Glory to God in the highest, And on earth peace, good will toward men." NKJV

It is a new way for me to pray and declare now. "All my children will be taught by the Lord and great will be their (Shalom) peace." Is. 54:13

How will I keep the peace? I will wear it on me daily, just as I wear the full armor of God, with His Word, and the Name of Jesus. That is how I carry it with me, because I want His peace to be with me daily!

"Lord, as I sit at your feet and learn of you, from pastors' or even from spending time with you, I pray some of this Shalom Peace would rub off, and be able to touch others, so each one could experience this peace. I thank You for being My Peace today."

◆ ◆ ◆

*Discussion moments*
*What does Shalom peace mean to you?*
*How will you keep the peace?*

But wait, there is more!

The Lord said to Moses, Tell Aaron and his sons, this is how you are to bless the Israelites, Say to them:

*"The Lord bless you*
*and keep you;*
*the Lord make his face shine upon you*
*and be gracious to you;*
*the Lord turn his face*
*toward you*
*and give you peace,*

So, they will put my name on the Israelites, and I will bless them." Numbers 6:22-27 NIV

(His Name is Jehovah Shalom and they were declaring this verse over Israel)

I want His Name (Jehovah Shalom) to be on me, so that I will be blessed with Peace too ! Don't you?

# I WILL IF YOU WILL

**M**r. Kerr was a believer in Christ. He lived in the early 1900's. He was skeptical at first about tithing when he learned about Malachi 3:7-11 "Will a man rob God? Yet you have robbed Me! But you say, 'In what way have we robbed You?' In tithes and offerings. You are cursed with a curse, for you have robbed Me, Even this whole nation. Bring all the tithe into the storehouse, that there may be food in My house, and try Me now in this," Says the Lord of hosts, "If I will not open for you the windows of heaven and pour out for you such blessing that there will not be room enough to receive it. And I will rebuke the devourer for your sakes, so that he will not destroy the fruit of your ground, nor shall the vine fail to bear fruit for you in the field, Says the Lord of hosts;" NKJV

After trying it for few months, Mr. Kerr began to see a difference. He owned the Kerr Glass Manufacturing Company, which sold the fruit canning jars. These jars were manufactured in San Francisco, California. Mr. Kerr had invested all his money into this fruit jar business. In 1906 there was an earthquake in San Francisco, and then a fire. The people who knew Mr. Kerr told him that he probably lost everything. He knew that God is a promise keeper, and he was holding onto that promise.

Mr. Kerr tried to find out what was going on in San Francisco. He sent a telegram and waited. The reply told him that the factory was right in the middle of the fire and was probably destroyed. They had to wait a few days for everything to cool down. Mr. Kerr was standing on God's Word in Malachi 3:11 "I will rebuke the devourer for your sakes, and he shall not destroy the fruit of your ground."

Then about a week after the earthquake and fire, Mr. Kerr received another telegram that informed him that everything within a mile and a half around the factory had burned, but his factory was saved, not a glass jar broken or cracked by the earthquake or the fire. This factory was a wooden building which housed a lot of flammable product to make the glass jars at high heating temperatures. It should have burned, but God kept His promise to Mr. Kerr.

Just the thought of glass jars in an earthquake would make most people think there can be no way that business survived. It was such a fantastic miracle!

I will if you will, is how God answered. Mr. Kerr was doing his part, by tithing and believing God's Word. He stood his ground when the circumstances were against him. It is a true story. God did His part and saved his business from devastation. I heard this story many years ago and it stuck with me.

The Word is still relevant today. What a great promise we have as we tithe, not only will He pour out a great blessing upon us, but also rebuke the devourer off us, so that what belongs to us will not be destroyed. There will be no curse on us!

"I thank you Lord that I am a tither today, and I ask you to rebuke the devourer off my finances, off my vehicles, off my home and all of my property, everything that belongs to me, and my job or business. Even though maintenance needs to be done on things, I pray that it will not be as expensive to repair, because there no longer is any curse on me, or my finances or anything that belongs to me! According to your Word, Lord, as it will not return to you void, but will accomplish what you have called it to do."

I admit there have been times when I have forgotten this promise and failed to stand up when my finances came under attack. The car breaks down, the washing machine quits working, then a medical problem all in the same month. As a believer in Christ there is still redemption.

The Lord says that He will restore to you all the years the locust has eaten. Joel 2:25 So even though you have paid tithes for years, and maybe had a decrease instead of an increase, you can still declare His Word over you and ask Him to redeem that which was lost or stolen from you! Ask the Lord to rebuke the devourer off you because you are a tither! If that is you also, ask the Lord, If He will restore to you, all the years the locust has eaten as His Word says. Forgive me for not standing on your Word!

*Discussion moments*
*What do you think about tithing?*
*What would you have done?*

# MY REFUGE

Psalm 91

Those who live in the shelter of the Most High, will find rest in the shadow of the Almighty. This I declare about the Lord: He alone is my refuge, my place of safety; He is my God, and I trust him. For he will rescue you from every trap and protect you from deadly disease. He will cover you with his feathers. He will shelter you with his wings. His faithful promises are your armor and protection. Do not be afraid of the terrors of the night, nor the arrow that flies in the day. Do not dread the disease that stalks in darkness, nor the disaster that strikes at midday. Though a thousand fall at your side, though ten thousand are dying around you, these evils will not touch you. Just open your eyes, and you will see how the wicked are punished. If you make the Lord your refuge, if you make the Most High your shelter, no evil will conquer you; no plague will come near your home. For he will order his angels to protect you wherever you go. They will hold you up in their hands, so that you will not even hurt your foot on a stone. You will trample on lions and cobras; you will crush fierce lions under your feet! The Lord says, "I will rescue those who love me. I will protect those who trust in my name. When they call on me, I will answer; I will be with them in trouble. I will rescue and honor them. I will reward them with a long life and give them my salvation." NLT

We can declare this whole Psalm! I will say the Lord is my refuge! I would rather run to Him, than away from Him when I am in trouble.

As the world is concerned with the different flu viruses and plagues happening around us, His Word is true and stays the same.

This Psalm goes along with the previous chapter titled "I Will if You Will." When we do our part, He will do His part for us. If you will declare the Lord is your refuge, then He will do what His Word says. Along with "no plague shall come near your home," "He will give His angels charge over you to keep you in all your ways" is the verse of protection that I use for myself and my family.

"Lord I declare today that you are my refuge. I declare your Word which says no plague shall come near my or my family's homes. No sickness disease or plague can trespass here. I declare it is you Lord who gives your angels charge over us to keep us in all our ways. I thank you Lord for sending your angels to protect us from all evil."

◆ ◆ ◆

*Discussion moments*
*What do you do when you are in trouble?*

# NOT ON MY
# WATCH!

I am writing this while the Covid-19 pandemic virus has come to the United States. I know that many are praying at this time, while fear has really hit most households because they do not really know what to do. Soon it will no longer be a headline, but maybe a learning experience. What did you do during the pandemic of 2020?

Of course, naturally I prayed and made declarations every day for myself and my family, mostly Psalm 91, and others about healing and the blood of Jesus. But when it became a worldwide pandemic, I thought that we needed to start praying differently. I asked the Lord how should I be praying now?

There was a verse in the bible that kept popping

into my head and that verse mentioned the enemy coming in like a flood and the Lord would raise a standard against him. I looked it up, it does not read the same in the NIV, compared to the KJV or NKJV. It is one of those verses that got lost in translation. Isaiah 59:19 "So shall they fear the name of the Lord from the west, And His glory from the rising of the sun; When the enemy comes in like a flood, The Spirit of the Lord will lift up a standard against him." NKJV The moment I spoke that scripture verse out loud, I felt the power come out of my mouth as I spoke it. It was like a rhema word to me. I have never used this scripture before, but I have read it. I have only a few times felt a powerful word when I have prayed or said something spiritual, which does not happen all the time. I believed that was my answer as to how to pray at this time.

The enemy was coming in like a flood, and the Lord is going to fight this battle for us! I started to declare that verse, also Jehovah Nissi as one of the Names of God. Exodus 17:9-15 When Moses and the Israelites were fighting against the Amalekites, he raised his rod high and the Israelites prevailed, and when his arms grew tired and would go down, the Amalekites prevailed. Aaron and Hur supported his hands until the sun went down when Joshua defeated the Amalekites. Moses then built an altar and called it, "THE LORD IS MY BANNER." Jehovah Nissi is the Hebrew version. During battles they would use flags as a rallying point to gather and give information for the battle.

I asked the Lord to fight this battle for us and told Him that He was my Hero, my Champion! It was a time to cheer Him on because the victory is His. He has won all the battles. We just need to give Him the battle and be His cheerleaders! That is the only way that I know how to describe what that verse means. He is the One who will protect us and help give those of authority over us to make decisions, helping doctors to come up with the right anti-virus prescriptions to help the sick and help take the fear off the people as we put our hope, faith and trust in Him! Wisdom about the financial problems involved with most people out of work.

Within a few days of praying differently, I went to a woman's prayer breakfast in Battle Creek. We did not have the breakfast due to safety and prevention orders being put into place along with being told that we would have to limit the amounts of people gathering. Some of the Pastor's wives came on stage and prayed for the women who gathered for the meeting. One of the first things which came out of one lady's mouth was, "Jehovah Nissi is one of the names of God. Always know who God is, and always know who you are." That was confirmation to me of what I had been praying about.

During those hard times we are hopefully having an

attitude of not allowing the enemy to prevail, raising our banners high and declaring the Lord is able to win, just as we would cheer for our favorite athletic team. Sons and Daughters of the King let us get that attitude of "Not on our Watch" (the enemy will not prevail) for our families, our churches, our communities, our nations, our world! The Name of Jesus is still greater than any mountain we will ever face! His Name is greater than any disease! Let us cheer Him on before the battle is won!

As the battle and war was continuing, battle strategies tend to shift and change. I was wondering what the generals in the army of God, the apostles and prophets were saying about all of this. They had mentioned that 2020 was going to be a great year and revival was coming. One prophet mentioned there would be some things that we would have to fight for. Another prophet mentioned that a pandemic would be coming and would be done by Passover. You can find out what the prophets are saying by going online to the elijahlist.com. Many prophets post what the Lord has told them during this time.

It just happened that the President held a conference on the last day of Passover with the governors from each state and mentioned that he wanted to see the United States open again and each governor would be responsible for when.

I know that we were all doing everything that we possibly could to get rid of this virus pandemic. Many praying, many helping wherever they could, many on the front lines helping the sick, trying to save lives. If you lost someone during this time, I am so sorry! I pray the Holy Spirit will comfort you and give you peace.

My 85-year-old mother was in assisted living during this time. She was not feeling well and tested positive for covid-19. She was admitted to the hospital. My sister's and I prayed for her and released her to the Lord. I did not think she was going to make it since she was very weak and not eating. She needed assistance to eat and to get in and out of bed. She never needed a respirator and after two weeks she got out of the hospital and went back into assisted living. I believe that was a miracle that God spared her life and answered our prayers even during a time when the assisted living and senior living homes were hit the hardest with this pandemic! I did not want my mom to be one of the daily statistics. I was standing on Psalm 91 "No plague shall come near our dwelling, not on my watch!"

We needed to be humble at this time, and continue in prayer for our families, communities, cities, states and nations. 2 Chronicles 7:14 "If My people who are called by My name will humble themselves and pray and seek My face and turn from their wicked ways, then I will hear from heaven, and will forgive their sin and heal their land." NKJV

With all the prayers going out for wisdom, for health, and help, people came together in unexpected ways of sharing and caring amidst limited venues.

Through it all I learned something important. It is God who gives certain ones the strategic battle plans. The apostles and prophets carry the authority to cover the nation they are called to. They are like generals in the army of God, and they carry a powerful anointing. It would be wise for us to do what they are hearing the Lord say to do. Pastors carry authority also but usually just in their city. We all have a sphere of influence and authority. For most if us, it usually involves our family, friends, people we work with and our churches and neighbors. It is best for us to pray within our sphere of influence.

Going back to the original scripture verse, Isaiah 59:19 "So shall they fear the name of the Lord from the west, And His glory from the rising of the sun: When the enemy comes in like a flood, The Spirit of the Lord will lift up a standard against him." NKJV It is interesting that this verse states they shall (respect) fear the name of the Lord from the west. The earth rotates from east to west and the sun rises from the east and sets in the west. So unusual for something to start in the west. The Lord has fought this battle for us, and great miracles will take place. I still declared this verse and expected revival, restoration, and restitution to come out of this.

Joel 2:28 "And afterward, I will pour out my Spirit on all people, your sons and daughters will prophesy, your old men will dream dreams, your young men will see visions. Even on my servants, both men and women, I will pour out my spirit in these days." NIV

"Even so as your Word says, pour out the fullness of your spirit in these last days, send us revival, signs and wonders, miracles!"

❖ ❖ ❖

*Discussion moments*
*What did you do during the pandemic of 2020?*
*What did you learn from it?*

# PSALM 23

The Lord is my shepherd; I shall not want. He makes me to lie down in green pastures;

He leads me beside the still waters,

He restores my soul; He leads me in the paths of righteousness for His name's sake.

Yea, though I walk through the valley of the shadow of death,

I will fear no evil; for You are with me;

Your rod and your staff they comfort me.

You prepare a table before me in the presence of my enemies;

You anoint my head with oil; my cup runs over.

Surely goodness and mercy will follow me all the days of my life;

And I will dwell in the house of the Lord forever. NKJV

"Lord, I thank you today that you are my shepherd and because you are my shepherd I shall not want. You are such a great provider to me. You have made provision for me in small ways and in huge ways.

I thank you for restoring my soul today. You are the one who restores relationships with friends and family. You also restore my mind and my body. I receive that today.

Sometimes I get ahead of you and end up going the wrong way. Forgive me for being impatient. Please keep me on your path and let me walk beside you.

Sometimes I have lagged behind, and maybe even gotten lost. I really want to hear your voice, so please help me to stay close to you. That is why your rod and staff comfort me. I know that you are always right there, helping me, guiding me. Take the hook part of your staff when I am going the wrong way or just being stubborn. I need you!

I will fear no evil because you are my protector. You are always there, walking beside me every day.

I want to walk along the path that you have designed for me to walk upon so that I can fulfill the purposes that you created me for. Help me to stay within the boundary of your path. Sometimes I have jumped over the boundary and made some big mistakes. I appreciate that you are my maker and creator. I revere you and want to honor you!

I thank you for preparing a table for me in the presence of my enemies. Even though I have made mistakes, I repented of my sins and I am thankful that you would honor me by preparing a table for me in the presence of my enemies. I thank you for your favor over me today.

I thank you for anointing my head with oil today! I thank you for your anointing over me today that helps give me the strength to do your will. I am overflowing with it!

Surely your goodness and mercy will chase me down and catch me all the days of my life. Thank you for all the blessings!

And I will dwell in the house of the Lord forever. The promise of living with you forever. To have a place to go when my time here on earth is done is such a great promise to me!"

Thank you for being my shepherd today!

*Discussion moments*

*Have you recognized the Lord as shepherd in your life?*

# THE BLACK SHEEP

Have you known someone, or maybe it is you, who felt like the black sheep of the family? This person who does not seem to fit in with the rest of us. They tend to do things their own way instead of following the rules and end up making huge mistakes and messes in their lives.

I know that I for one have been there. I have made some massive mistakes. As the saying goes, "It takes one to know one." I have felt like the black sheep at times. Let me say there is nothing racial to this story, so let us not go there. No offense, the black sheep is a metaphor. Basically, the rebels, prodigals and misfits are who I am referring to.

For some of us, we have been labeled as the black sheep of the family, or a pain in the rear end, because of the messes we have made.

Let us look at the story of Jabez in 1 Chron. 4:9-10 "Now Jabez was more honorable than his brothers, and is mother called him Jabez, saying, "Because I bore him in pain." And Jabez called on the God of Israel, saying, "Oh that you would bless me indeed and enlarge my territory, that your hand would be with me, and that you would keep me from evil, that I may not cause pain." So, God granted him what he requested. NKJV

There are only a few sentences here in the Bible with no references, so it is a gray area left to our own interpretation. The following is my interpretation.

The word Jabez means will cause pain or sorrow in the Hebrew language. Jabez was labeled a "pain" from birth. His mom probably had complications during labor. It must have been excruciatingly painful. They did not have the knowledgeable doctors or the equipment which we have now.

But can you imagine being called pain every day? The constant shame and ridicule that he had to live with? Whenever he made a mistake his brothers would probably tell him that he was just living up to his name. Layers and layers of condemnation and judgement from the family and possibly the community.

Recently I had to find a new dentist. On the list was a Dr. Pain, which I crossed off that one right away. Just the thought of dentist and pain because of some bad experiences I have had. But look at my reaction to that name.

I think that Jabez was the black sheep of the family. I believe he got into some evil in order to pray such a deep sincere prayer, or why would he ask God to keep him from evil? One day he must have looked at his life. He was not asking his family to bless him. Usually, the oldest or first born received the blessing from the parents. He probably was a middle child or maybe the youngest. Jabez probably came to a point of realizing that he needed a life change.

When Jabez called on the God of Israel, he had a divine encounter with God. There was probably forgiveness involved. He did not want to be the cause of pain people's pain any longer. He wanted to be something better maybe a blessing instead of a pain.

It is so hard to rise above the condemning words spoken against us, but it is God who can break through after we have a sincere moment with Him. Because of the great grace of God, the latter part of Jabez's life was better than the beginning. He had a divine appointment with the God of Israel who heard his prayer, answered and blessed him. It changed his life!

I think it is time for us to forgive the black sheep and ask God to bring them back to the sheepfold.

Jer. 31:16-17 This is what the Lord says: "Restrain your voice from weeping and your eyes from tears, for your work will be rewarded, Declares the Lord. "They will return from the land of the enemy. So, there is hope for your future." Declares the Lord. "Your children will return to their own land."

Lord your word says that these children will return from the land of the enemy and we want them to come back. We forgive them and we want them to forgive us. Please bring back all the prodigals and black sheep.

TINA DOWNER

◆ ◆ ◆

*Discussion moments*

*Do you have any black sheep in your family?*

*What kind of a sheep are you?*

# ACKNOWLEDGEMENT

There have been many Pastors over the years who have impacted my life who I would like to thank.

Pastor Paul and Bonnie Booko and Pastor John Booko of Riverside Church, Three Rivers Michigan. I grew so much in your church through various teachings and small group ministries. I love your heart to serve the community and I love being a part of it!

Apostle Dutch Sheets Colorado Springs, Colorado. While I attended your church in Colorado I learned of spiritual authority.

Larry and Vicky McKnight of Joyland Church, Green Mountain Falls, Colorado. I learned more about God's creativeness!

Apostle Robert Henderson Colorado Springs, Colorado. I learned many things about the power of God

and the courts of heaven.
Thank you all so much! I could not have written this book if you did not take the time to teach. I feel that some of your teachings have rubbed off on me!

# ABOUT THE AUTHOR

## Tina Downer

Tina found a new way to pray with authority when doing her family geneology and realizing that she carries a title as one of the "daughters of the king." Through multiple near death experiences , divorce, single-parenting and loss of a husband and father in the same year, she portrays stories of faith and hope about the answers to many different prayer situations.

Made in the USA
Monee, IL
28 October 2021